THE SURPRISING THINGS MAUI DID

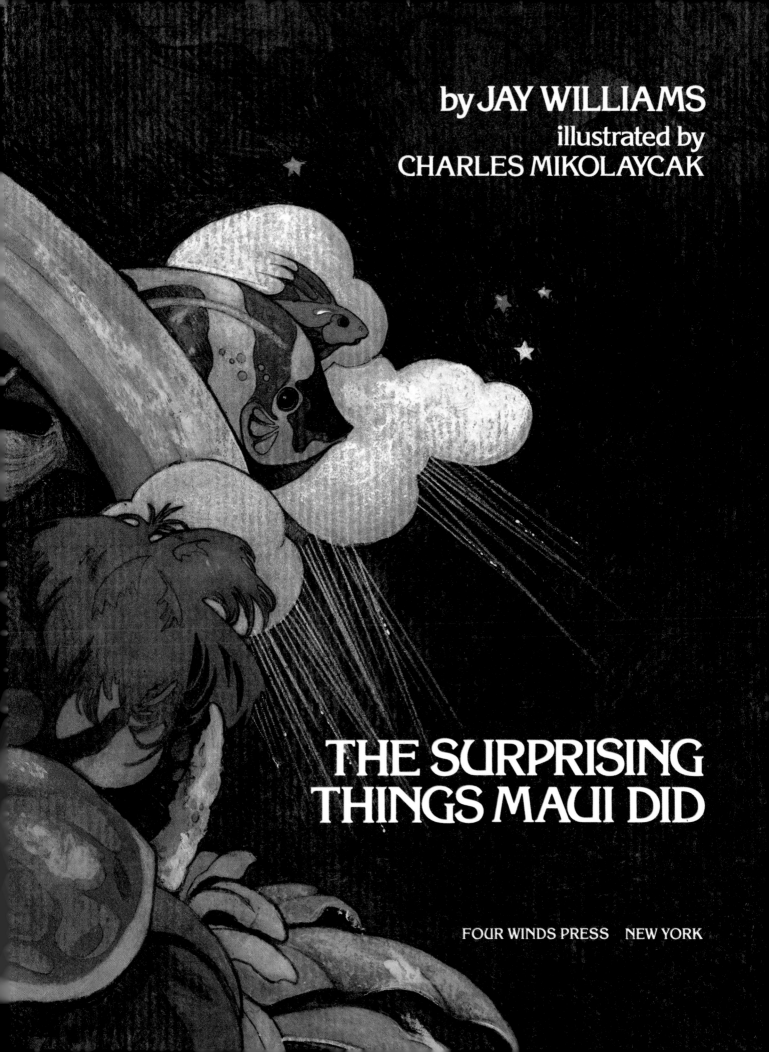

by JAY WILLIAMS
illustrated by
CHARLES MIKOLAYCAK

THE SURPRISING
THINGS MAUI DID

FOUR WINDS PRESS   NEW YORK

LIBRARY OF CONGRESS CATALOGING IN PUBLICATION DATA

Williams, Jay.
    The surprising things Maui did.

    Summary: Relates a young Hawaiian boy's many extraordinary
deeds that changed the lives of his neighbors.
        I. Maui (Polynesian deity)—Juvenile literature.
        [1. Maui (Polynesian deity)
    2. Mythology, Polynesian] I. Mikolaycak, Charles. II. Title.
PZ8.1.W652Sp   398.2′1′0996[E]   79-5069
ISBN 0-590-07553-5

PUBLISHED BY FOUR WINDS PRESS
A DIVISION OF SCHOLASTIC MAGAZINES, INC., NEW YORK, N.Y.
TEXT COPYRIGHT © 1979 BY BARBARA G. WILLIAMS
ILLUSTRATIONS COPYRIGHT © 1979 BY CHARLES MIKOLAYCAK
ALL RIGHTS RESERVED
PRINTED IN THE UNITED STATES OF AMERICA
LIBRARY OF CONGRESS CATALOG CARD NUMBER: 79-5069
1 2 3 4 5 83 82 81 80 79

Long ago, things were different. The people who lived on the islands of Hawaii and Oahu and Molokai and all the other islands that lay upon the Great Sea were poor and hungry, cold and sad. Then, there came a boy named Maui who changed everything. This is how it happened.

His mother was named Hina, and although she was married to an ordinary man, her brother was the God of the Sea. She had five sons and five daughters, and when Maui was born the crops failed and there was very little food. So Hina wrapped up the baby and took him to the shore, and called to the God of the Sea to take care of him. The Sea God came and carried Maui away to his own land. There, in the land under the waves, Maui grew tall and strong, stronger than anyone else. But because he swam around all day in the green waters, he became very lazy.

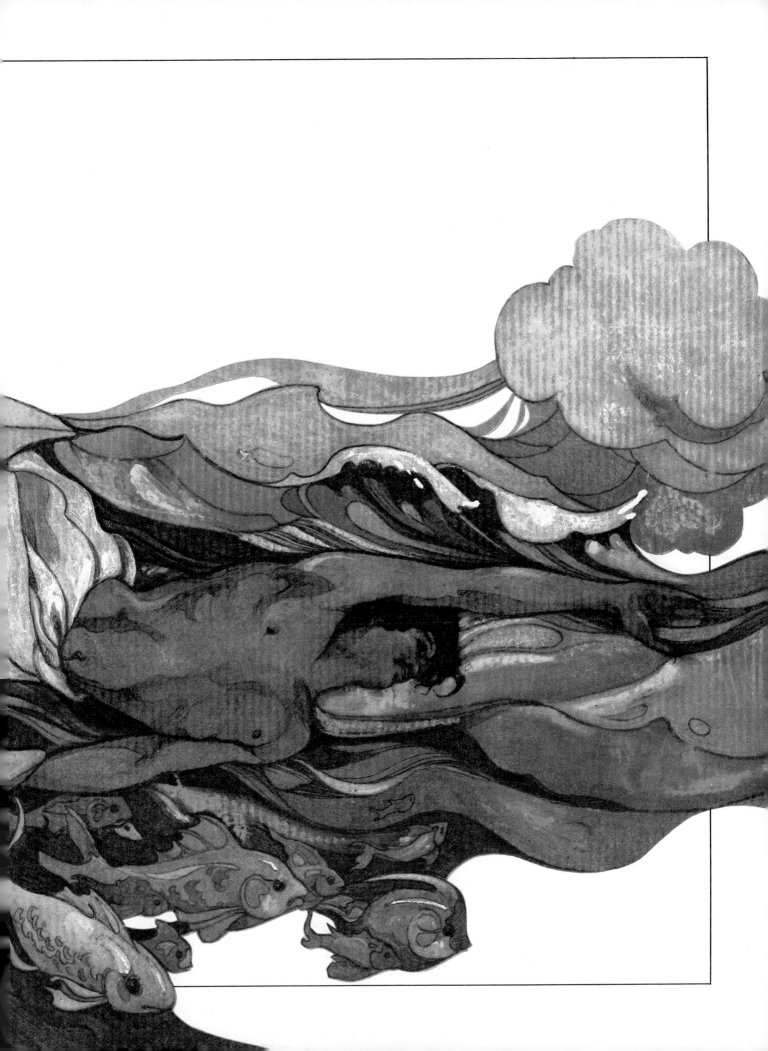

After some years, the Sea God learned that there was food again, on the land, and he sent Maui home. Maui walked up out of the waves, and there was his own house with its thatched roof, and outside were his five brothers. They were throwing toy spears at the roof. The spears stuck in the hatch. It looked like a good game, so Maui made a spear and threw it at the roof, too. It went through one side of the roof and through the house and out the other side.

Out came Hina to see who had done such a thing. As soon as she saw her youngest son, she recognized him. She wept and hugged him, and led him to the house to give him some dinner. At the doorway, there were two enormous posts which guarded the house. They were called Tall Post and Short Post. Now when Maui had walked as far as the doorway, he felt tired, so he leaned against Tall Post. It cracked and fell down. Then he leaned against Short Post. It splintered and fell down.

Everyone thought that that was a surprising thing for a boy his age to do. But Maui only said, "Now there is more room for me to go in and out."

He settled down and lived happily with his mother and his brothers and his sisters, glad to be home. But his brothers complained because Maui never did any work, but lay dozing on the beach all day, or swam in the sea.

In those days, long ago, things were different: there were no birds. One day, a man came from a faraway place called Kahiki-mo-e. Everyone made him welcome, and when he had feasted he told them all about the land he had come from. Everything there, according to him, was more beautiful than anywhere else. The flowers were lovelier, the crops better, the mountains higher. After a while, he stopped talking long enough to catch his breath.

Maui was lying with his back against a tree. He yawned and stretched, and then he took out a little drum and began to play it. From the trees, small voices answered his drum. They sang more sweetly than any music anyone had ever heard. Maui clapped his hands, and at once the birds appeared, the sweet singers with their brilliant feathers. They flew about from tree to tree like flowers with voices.

The man from Kahiki-mo-e went home without saying anything more. But the birds remained and they are still there.

In those days, long ago, things were different: the sky was very low. It rested on the tops of the trees and flattened them, and squashed the leaves. It made the world very dark and sad.

One day, Maui's brothers looked at him lying on the beach, and said, "You are too lazy. Why don't you do something useful for a change?"

Maui sat up and yawned. First, he went into the house and ate all the food he could find there. When he came outside, he rubbed his hands together and loosened up the muscles of his arms. He jumped up and down to loosen the muscles of his legs. Then he climbed to the top of the tallest tree.

Standing on its top, he reached up until he was touching the sky. He pushed with all his might, and slowly the sky began to lift. He pushed and pushed, and the sky was shoved higher and higher until at last it was where it is now. But the leaves of the palm trees had been squashed so flat that they couldn't straighten up, and they are still flat.

"I have done enough work for one day," said Maui, and went back to sleep.

In those days, long ago, things were different: the sun went across the sky very swiftly. Daylight only lasted a few hours so that farmers couldn't grow their crops very well, and fishermen had very little time to fish. Maui's mother, Hina, complained that she didn't have enough daylight to make her tapacloth.

So Maui watched the sun, and he saw that every morning it came from a hole in the great mountain called Halea-kala. The sun ran up to the mountain top and stopped for a few minutes at a wiliwili tree. An old woman lived near there, and every morning she baked bananas for the sun's breakfast. When the sun had eaten, it raced across the sky and dived into the sea.

Maui wove together the strongest vines he could find, and made ropes. He made a net of the ropes, and took a stone club, and began to climb the mountain. He climbed to the wiliwili tree and hid himself in a cave under its roots.

The next morning, the sun came up. It ran to the mountain top and stopped at the tree. The old woman had put out the cooked bananas and the sun began to eat. Out jumped Maui and threw his net over the sun. He held it fast in the net and began to pound it with his club. At first, the sun struggled; then it began to cry hot tears and begged for mercy.

"I will let you go if you will move more slowly across the sky," said Maui.

The sun agreed. But Maui was kindhearted. He said that for six months of the year the sun must go slowly so that the land would be warm and the days would be longer. But for six months it could run as quickly as it had before, and that is how it moves to this day.

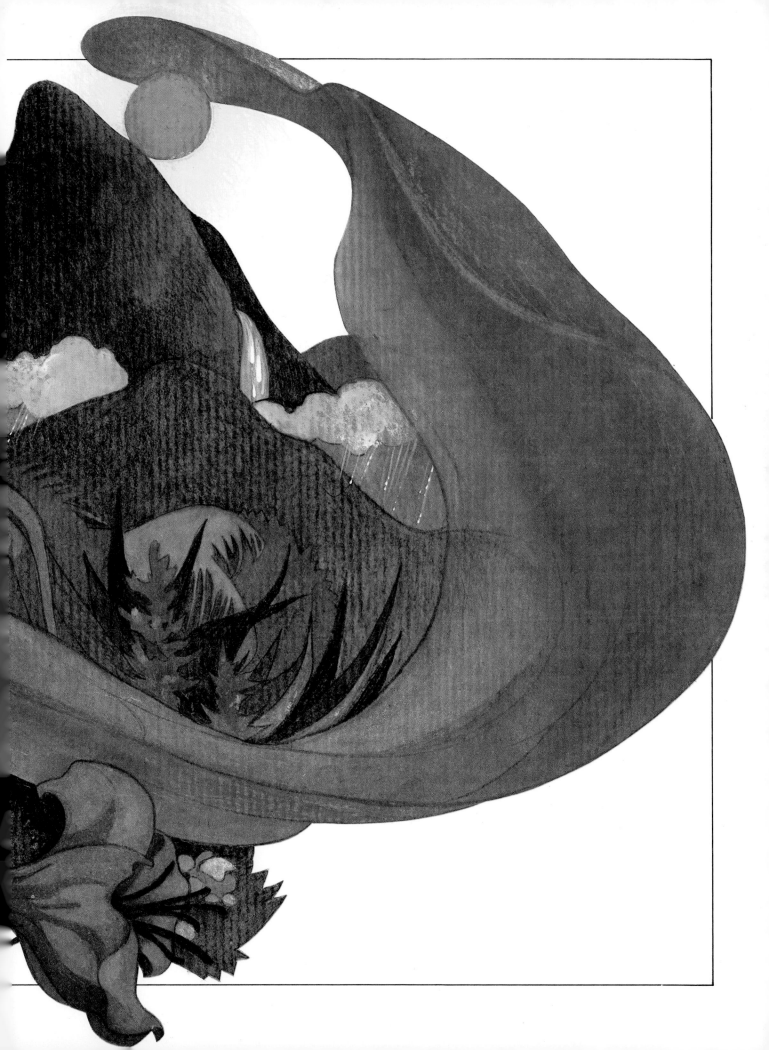

In those days, long ago, things were different: there was not enough room for all the people who lived on the islands in the sea. They were crowded together, and they wished for more land to live on.

One day, Maui's brothers jeered at him because he never went fishing with them. So Maui got up, and dusted the sand off himself, and scratched his head. Then he went into the house and got out a fishing line and a hook made of bone, that had been given to him by his uncle, the Sea God. He got into the canoe with his brothers, and told them to paddle him far out to sea.

"We will take you as far as you like," they said, grinning at each other. "Maybe you will catch a minnow."

When they were far out among the tossing waves, Maui baited his hook and dropped it over the side. He waited and waited, and his brothers began to get restless. Suddenly, the line tightened.

"Aha! I have caught something," said Maui. "Now paddle as hard as you can, but don't look back."

The brothers were surprised, but they bent to their paddling while Maui tugged at the line. Something came up, breaking the surface of the water, but it was not a fish. It was the top of a mountain.

Then came more peaks, and tall trees, and shrubs, and grass, until a whole island lay there. Just then, the brothers looked back to see what was happening. When they saw the island Maui had fished up, they became so frightened that they cut the line.

"Too bad," said Maui. "If you hadn't cut the line, I would have pulled up a whole country."

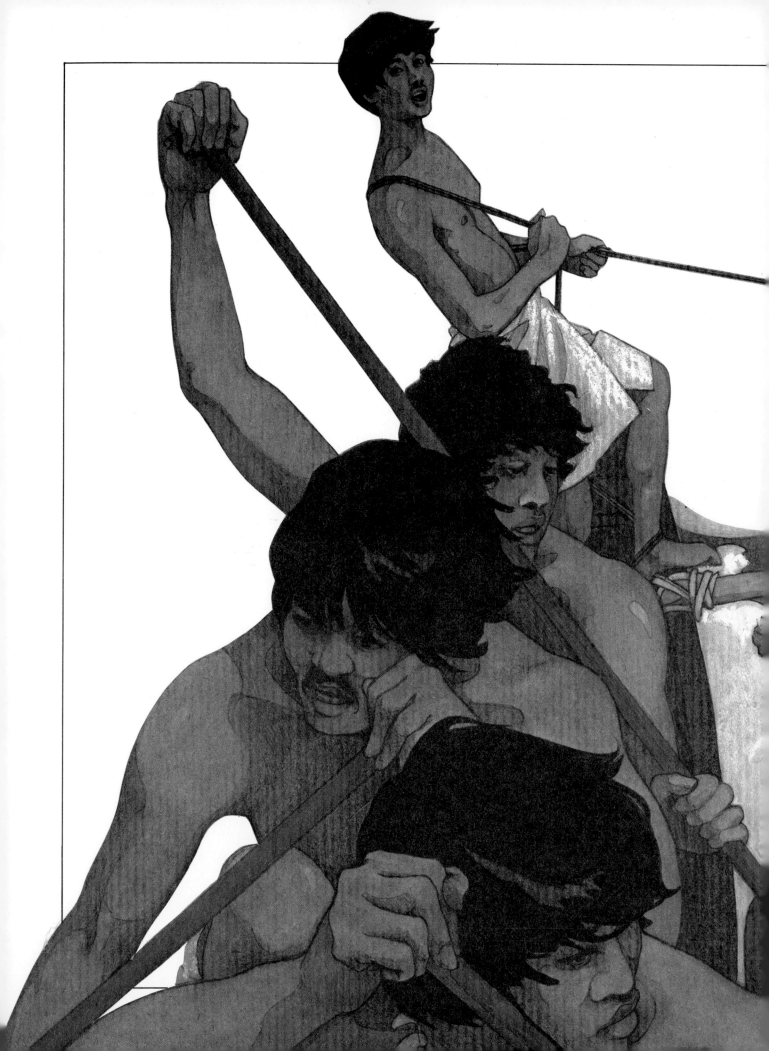

In those days, long ago, things were different: no one knew how to make a fire. People ate their food raw, or climbed a long hard road up to a volcano to cook their dinners in its fires.

Maui's brothers took turns carrying food up to the volcano for their mother, Hina. One day, they said to Maui, "If you weren't so lazy, you'd take a turn."

"I would rather bring some fire down here," said Maui.

He got up and went for a walk to think about it. On the top of a high cliff there was a forest, and among the trees he saw a thread of smoke. Some birds lived there, the ala-e, or mudhens.

Maui climbed the cliff, but when he got to the top the birds had flown away. He looked around. He could see that they had built a fire there, but when they heard him coming they had scratched dirt over it to put it out.

He went down to the house again. He took some tapacloth and rolled it up and tied it so that it looked like a person. He put it in the canoe and told his brothers to paddle out across the breakers as if they were going fishing. Then he quietly climbed the cliff again.

The birds had come back and were watching the canoe. The chief of the mudhens counted the figures in the canoe, and said, "I count five people paddling and one sitting in the middle. The five paddlers are Maui's brothers, and the sixth one must be lazy Maui. Now that he has gone, we can build our fire again."

The mudhens began to make a fire. From his hiding place, Maui could not see what they were doing. So he leaped out, and before they could fly away he caught the chief by the neck.

"Teach me how to make a fire!" said Maui.

The chief of the mudhens tried to get away, but Maui held him tightly. At last, the chief said, "You must rub two banana leaves together."

Maui tied the wings of the chief so that the bird could not fly away. He rubbed two banana leaves together, but nothing happened except that they grew soggy.

"You are lying," said Maui. "Tell me the truth."

"Very well," said the bird. "Rub two reeds together."

Maui tried that, but the reeds only broke. He took the bird by the neck and said, "If you will not tell me the truth, I'll throw you into the sea and the Sea God will eat you for dinner."

The bird squeaked with fear, and said, "Take two pieces of wood from the sandalwood tree and rub them together."

Maui did so. Fire sprang from the sticks.

Maui untied the wings of the chief and let him go. But before the bird flew off, Maui hit him on the head with one of the blazing sticks and to this day the mudhens all have streaks of red on their heads. Then Maui climbed down the cliff and brought the secret of how to make fire to the people below.

Maui grew up and lived for a long time, and then he went away. Nobody knows where he went. But there are the birds, and the sun going its rounds, and the high sky overhead, and the dancing of flames, and the island pulled out of the waves, and when they see them, the people of Hawaii and Oahu and Molokai and all the other islands remember the surprising things Maui did.

for Carole —